THE DESERT OF THE HEART

Daily Readings with the Desert Fathers

Introduced and edited by
Benedicta Ward SLG

SLG Press
Convent of the Incarnation
Fairacres Parker Street
Oxford OX4 1TB
UK
www.slgpress.co.uk

ISBN 978-0-7283-0290-7 (Paper)
ISBN 978-0-7283-0291-4 (ePub)
ISBN 978-0-7283-0292-1 (Kindle)
ISSN 0307-1405

First published in 1988 by Darton, Longman and Todd Ltd in the *Enfolded in Love* series.

Cover Picture: From left to right, Onophrius the Anchorite, Abba Macarius, Abba Apollo and Abba Poemen. Wall painting from the Monastery of Abba Jeremiah, Saqqara, Egypt, 6th–7th century, now in the Coptic Museum, Cairo.

*In loving and grateful remembrance
of my sister Marjorie and
of our parents, Florence and Oswald Ward*

Contents

Introduction

In the desert of the heart
Let the healing fountain start,
In the prison of his days
Teach the free man how to praise.[1]

In the fourth century, an intensive experiment in Christian living began to flourish in Egypt, Syria and Palestine. It was something new in Christian experience, uniting ancient forms of monastic life with the Gospel. In Egypt the movement was soon so popular that both the civil authorities and the monks themselves became anxious: the officials of the Empire because so many were following a way of life that excluded both military service and the payment of taxes, and the monks because the number of interested tourists threatened their solitude.

The first Christian monks tried every kind of experiment with the way they lived and prayed, but there were three main forms of monastic life: in Lower Egypt there were hermits who lived alone; in Upper Egypt there were monks and nuns living in communities; and in Nitria and Scetis there were those who lived solitary lives but in groups of three or four, often as disciples of a master. For the most part they were simple men, peasants from the villages by the Nile; though a few, like Arsenius and Evagrius, were well educated. Visitors who were impressed and moved by the life of the monks imitated their way of life as far as they could, and also provided a literature that explained and analysed this way of life for those outside it. However, the primary written accounts of the monks of Egypt are not these, but records of their words and actions by their close disciples.

---

[1] W. H. Auden, 'In Memory of W. B. Yeats,' from *Collected Shorter Poems 1927–1957*, Faber and Faber 1966, p. 143.

Often, the first thing that struck those who heard about the Desert Fathers was the negative aspect of their lives. They were people who did without: not much sleep, no baths, poor food, little company, ragged clothes, hard work, no leisure, absolutely no sex, and even, in some places, no church either—a dramatic contrast of immediate interest to those who lived out the Gospel differently.

But to read their own writings is to form a rather different opinion. The literature produced among the monks themselves is not very sophisticated; it comes from the desert, from the place where the amenities of civilization were at their lowest point anyway, where there was nothing to mark a contrast in lifestyles; and the emphasis is less on what was lacking and more on what was present. The outsider saw the negations; however, disciples who encountered the monks through their own words and actions found indeed great austerity and poverty, but it was neither unbelievable nor complicated. These were simple, practical men, not given either to mysticism or to theology, living by the Word of God, the love of the brethren and of all creation, waiting for the coming of the Kingdom with eager expectation, using each moment as a step in their pilgrimage of the heart towards Christ.

It was because of this positive desire for the Kingdom of Heaven which came to dominate their whole lives that they went without things. They kept silence, for instance, not because of a proud and austere preference for aloneness but because they were learning to listen to something more interesting than the talk of men, that is, the Word of God. These men were rebels, the ones who broke the rules of the world which say that property and goods are essential for life, that the one who accepts the direction of another is not free, that no one can be fully human without sex and domesticity. Their name itself, anchorite, means rule-breaker, the one who does not fulfil his public duties. In the solitude of the desert they found themselves able to live in a way that was hard but simple, as children of God.

The literature they have left behind is full of a good, perceptive wisdom, from a clear, unassuming angle. They did not write much. Most of them remained illiterate; but they asked each other for a 'word', that is, to say something in which they would recognize the Word of God, which gives life to the soul. It is not a literature of words that analyse and sort out personal worries or solve theological problems; nor is it a mystical literature concerned to present prayers and praise to God in a direct line of vision; rather, it is oblique, unformed, occasional, like sunlight glancing off a rare oasis in the sands.

These life-giving 'words' were collected and eventually written down by disciples of the first monks, and grouped together in various ways, sometimes under the names of the monks with whom they were connected, sometimes under headings which were themes of special interest, such as 'solitude and stability', 'obedience' or 'the warfare that lust arouses in us'. Mixed in with these sayings were short stories about the actions of the monks, since what they did was often as revealing as what they said. These collections of 'apophthegmata' were not meant as a dead archaism, full of nostalgia for a lost past, but as a direct transmission of practical wisdom and experience for the use of the reader. Thus it is as part of a tradition that this small selection has been made from some of the famous collections of desert material, most of which have been translated and published in full elsewhere. They are placed in pairs, so that a 'word' is followed by a story which illustrates its central, though not its only, meaning. Each saying-and-story pair has been given a heading; these are arranged in two series, the first part relating to the commandment to love one's neighbour, the second to the commandment to love God.

This material first appeared among uneducated laymen; it is not 'churchy' or specifically religious. It has its roots in that life in Christ which is common to all the baptized, some of whom lived this out as monks, others who did not. There is a universal appeal in these sayings, in spite of much which is at first strange. I have not tried to eliminate all the strangeness of the material, but to present a very small part of it as it is, in the belief that the words and deeds of these men and women can still make the fountain of life spring up in the arid deserts of lives in the twenty-first century as they did in the fourth. 'Fear not this goodness', said abba Antony, 'as a thing impossible, nor the pursuit of it as something alien, set a great way off; it hangs on our own choice. For the sake of Greek learning, men go overseas ... But the City of God has its foundations in every seat of human habitation ... The Kingdom of God is within ... The goodness that is in us asks only the human mind.'[2]

EDITOR'S NOTE

I have retained the words 'abba' and 'amma' which are used in these texts for addressing and describing certain men and women of the desert; 'abba' is a term of respect, and to translate it by 'abbot' would be misleading.

BENEDICTA WARD SLG
Oxford

---

[2] Athanasius, 'Life of St Antony', in *Early Christian Lives*, tr. Caroline White, Penguin Classics 1998, p. 22.

A Prayer from the Desert

Lord Jesus Christ, whose will all things obey: pardon what I have done and grant that I, a sinner, may sin no more. Lord, I believe that though I do not deserve it, you can cleanse me from all my sins. Lord, I know that man looks upon the face, but you see the heart. Send your Spirit into my inmost being, to take possession of my soul and body. Without you I cannot be saved; with you to protect me, I long for your salvation. And now I ask you for wisdom; deign of your great goodness to help and defend me. Guide my heart, almighty God, that I may remember your presence day and night.

Love of Others

Not to Judge

SAYINGS

The old men used to say, 'There is nothing worse than passing judgement.'

They said of abba Macarius that he became as it is written a god upon earth, because just as God protects the world, so abba Macarius would cover the faults that he saw as though he did not see them, and those which he heard as though he did not hear them.

Abba Pastor said, 'Judge not him who is guilty of fornication, if you are chaste, or you will break the law like him. For He who said "Do not commit fornication" said also "Do not judge".'

A brother asked abba Poemen, 'If I see my brother sin, is it right to say nothing about it?' The old man replied, 'Whenever we cover our brother's sin, God will cover ours; whenever we tell people about our brother's guilt, God will do the same about ours.'

STORIES

A brother in Scetis committed a fault. A council was called to which abba Moses was invited, but he refused to go to it. Then the priest sent someone to him, saying, 'Come, for everyone is waiting for you'. So he got up and went. He took a leaking jug and filled it with water and carried it with him. The others came out to meet him and said, 'What is this, father?' The old man said to them, 'My sins run out behind me, and I do not see them, and today I am coming to judge the errors of another.' When they heard that, they said no more to the brother but forgave him.

A brother sinned and the priest ordered him to go out of the church; abba Bessarion got up and went out with him, saying, 'I, too, am a sinner.'

True Peace

SAYINGS

One of the brothers asked abba Isidore, a priest of Scetis, 'Why are the demons so terrified of you?' And the old man said, 'Ever since I became a monk I have tried never to let anger rise as far as my mouth.'

Abba Joseph asked abba Nisteros, 'What should I do about my tongue, for I cannot control it?' The old man said to him, 'When you speak, do you find peace?' He replied, 'No.' The old man said to him, 'If you do not find peace, why do you speak? Be silent, and when a conversation takes place, prefer to listen rather than to talk.'

STORIES

Two old men had lived together for many years and they had never fought with one another. The first said to the other, 'Let us also have a fight like other men.' The other replied, 'I do not know how to fight.' The first said to him, 'Look, I will put a brick between us and I will say: it is mine; and you will reply: no, it is mine; and so the fight will begin.' So they put a brick between them and the first said, 'This brick is mine', and the other said, 'No, it is mine.' And the first replied, 'If it is yours, take it and go.' So they gave it up without being able to find a cause for an argument.

A brother asked abba Poemen, 'How should I behave in my cell in the place where I am living?' He replied, 'Behave as if you were a stranger, and wherever you are, do not expect your words to have any influence and you will be at peace.'

Obedience

SAYINGS

The holy Syncletica said, 'I think that for those living in community obedience is a greater virtue than chastity, however perfect. Chastity carries within it the danger of pride, but obedience has within it the promise of humility.'

The old men used to say, 'If someone has faith in another and hands himself over to him in complete submission, he does not need to pay attention to God's commandments but he can entrust his whole will to his father. He will suffer no reproach from God, for God looks for nothing from beginners so much as renunciation through obedience.'

Abba Mios of Belos said, 'Obedience responds to obedience. When someone obeys God, then God obeys his request.'

STORY

They said that abba Sylvanus had a disciple in Scetis named Mark, who possessed in great measure the virtue of obedience. He was a copyist of old manuscripts, and the old man loved him for his obedience. He had eleven other disciples who were aggrieved that he loved Mark more than them.

When the old men nearby heard that he loved Mark above the others, they took it ill. One day they visited him and abba Sylvanus took them with him and, going out of his cell, began to knock on the door of each of his disciples, saying, 'Brother, come out, I have work for you.' And not one of them appeared immediately.

Then he came to Mark's cell and knocked, saying, 'Mark'. And as soon as Mark heard the voice of the old man he came outside and the old man sent him on some errand.

So abba Sylvanus said to the old men, 'Where are the other brothers?' He went into Mark's cell and found the book in which he had been writing and he was making the letter O; and when he heard the old man's voice, he had not finished the line of the O.

And the old men said, 'Truly, abba, we also love the one whom you love; for God loves him, too.'

How to Become a Disciple

SAYINGS

Some old men said, 'If you see a young man climbing up to the heavens by his own will, catch him by the foot and throw him down to the earth; it is not good for him.'

At first abba Ammoe said to abba Isaiah, 'What do you think of me?' He said to him, 'You are an angel, father.' Later on he said to him, 'And now, what do you think of me?' He replied, 'You are like Satan. Even when you say a good word to me, it is like steel.'

Abba Moses asked abba Sylvanus, 'Can a man lay a new foundation every day?' The old man said, 'If he works hard, he can lay a new foundation at every moment.'

STORIES

It was said of abba John the Dwarf that one day he said to his elder brother, 'I should like to be free of all care, like the angels who do not work, but ceaselessly offer worship to God.' So he took leave of his brother and went away into the desert. After a week he came back to his brother. When he knocked on the door he heard his brother say, 'Who are you?' before he opened it. He said, 'I am John, your brother.' But he replied, 'John has become an angel and henceforth he is no longer among men.' Then John besought him, saying, 'It is I.' However, his brother did not let him in but left him there in distress until morning. Then, opening the door, he said to him, 'You are a man and you must once again work in order to eat.' Then John made a prostration before him, saying, 'Forgive me.'

Abba John said, 'A monk is toil. The monk toils in all he does. That is what a monk is.'

Humility

SAYINGS

An old man was asked, 'What is humility?' and he said in reply, 'Humility is a great work, and a work of God. The way of humility is to undertake bodily labour and believe yourself a sinner and make yourself subject to all.' Then a brother said, 'What does it mean, to be subject to all?' The old man answered, 'To be subject to all is not to give your attention to the sins of others but always to give your attention to your own sins and to pray without ceasing to God.'

An old man said, 'Every time a thought of superiority or vanity moves you, examine your conscience to see if you have kept all the commandments, whether you love your enemies, whether you consider yourself to be an unprofitable servant and the greatest sinner of all. Even so, do not pretend to great ideas as though you were perfectly right, for that thought destroys everything.'

STORIES

As abba Macarius was returning to his cell from the marsh carrying palm-leaves, the devil met him with a sharp sickle and would have struck him but he could not. He cried out, 'Great is the violence I suffer from you, Macarius, for when I want to hurt you, I cannot. But whatever you do, I do and more also. You fast now and then, but I am never refreshed by any food; you often keep vigil, but I never fall asleep. Only in one thing are you better than I am and I acknowledge that.' Macarius said to him, 'What is that?' and he replied, 'It is because of your humility alone that I cannot overcome you.'

The old men used to say, 'When we do not experience warfare, we ought so much the more to humiliate ourselves. For God seeing our weakness, protects us; when we glorify ourselves, he withdraws his protection and we are lost.'

True Poverty

SAYINGS

Abba Theodore, surnamed Pherme, had three good books. He went to abba Macarius and said to him, 'I have three good books, and I am helped by reading them; other monks also want to read them and they are helped by them. Tell me, what am I to do?' The old man said, 'Reading books is good but possessing nothing is more than all.' When he heard this, he went away and sold the books and gave the money to the poor.

Someone asked amma Syncletica of blessed memory, 'Is absolute poverty perfect goodness?' She replied, 'It is a great good for those capable of it; even those who are not capable of it find rest for their souls in it though it causes them anxiety. As tough cloth is laundered pure white by being stretched and trampled underfoot, so a tough soul is stretched by freely accepting poverty.'

STORIES

When abba Macarius was in Egypt, he found a man who had brought a beast to his cell and was stealing his possessions. He went up to the thief as though he were a traveller who did not live there and helped him to load the beast and led him on his way in peace, saying to himself, 'We brought nothing into this world; but the Lord gave; as he willed, so is it done; blessed be the Lord in all things.'

Someone brought money to an old man and said, 'Take this and spend it for you are old and ill', for he was a leper. The old man replied, 'Are you going to take me away from the One who has cared for me for sixty years? I have been ill all that time and I have not needed anything because God has cared for me.' And he would not accept it.

Once abba Arsenius fell ill in Scetis and in this state he needed just one coin. He could not find one so he accepted one as a gift from someone else, and he said, 'I thank you, God, that for your name's sake you have made me worthy to come to this pass, that I should have to beg.'

Life Together

SAYINGS

Amma Syncletica said, 'We ought to govern our souls with discretion and to remain in the community, neither following our own will nor seeking our own good. We are like exiles, for we have been separated from the things of this world and have given ourselves in one faith to the one Father. We need nothing of what we have left behind. There we had reputation and plenty to eat; here we have little to eat and little of everything else.'

Abba Antony said, 'Our life and our death are with our neighbour. If we gain our brother, we have gained our God; but if we scandalize our brother, we have sinned against Christ.'

A brother asked, 'I have found a place where my peace is not disturbed by the brethren; do you advise me to live there?' Abba Poemen replied, 'The place for you is where you will not harm the brothers.'

STORIES

There was an anchorite who was grazing with the antelopes and who prayed to God, saying, 'Lord, teach me something more.' And a voice came to him, saying, 'Go into this monastery and do whatever they tell you.' He went there and remained in the monastery, but he did not know the work of the brothers. The young monks began to teach him how to work and they would say to him, 'Do this, you idiot,' and 'Do that, you fool.' When he had borne it, he prayed to God, saying, 'Lord, I do not know the work of men; send me back to the antelopes.' And having been freed by God, he went back into the country to graze with the antelopes.

A beginner who goes from one monastery to another is like a wild animal that jumps this way and that for fear of the halter.

Silence

SAYINGS

Having withdrawn from the palace to the solitary life, abba Arsenius prayed and heard a voice saying to him, 'Arsenius, flee, be silent, pray always, for these are the source of sinlessness.'

A brother in Scetis went to ask for a word from abba Moses and the old man said to him, 'Go and sit in your cell and your cell will teach you everything.'

Abba Nilus said, 'The arrows of the enemy cannot touch one who loves quietness; but he who moves about in a crowd will often be wounded.'

STORIES

Theophilus of holy memory, bishop of Alexandria, journeyed to Scetis and the brethren coming together said to abba Pambo, 'Say a word or two to the bishop, that his soul may be edified in this place.' The old man replied, 'If he is not edified by my silence, there is no hope that he will be edified by my words.'

This place was called Cellia, because of the number of cells there, scattered about the desert. Those who have already begun their training there [i.e. in Nitria] and want to live a more remote life, stripped of external things, withdraw there. For this is the Utter Desert and the cells are divided from one another by so great a distance that no one can see his neighbour nor can any voice be heard. They live alone in their cells and there is a huge silence and a great quiet there. Only on Saturday and Sunday do they meet in church, and then they see each other face to face, as men restored to heaven.

The Kingdom Within

SAYINGS

It was revealed to abba Antony in his desert that there was one in the city who was his equal. He was a doctor by profession, and whatever he had beyond his needs he gave to the poor and every day he sang the *Sanctus* with the angels.

Amma Matrona said, 'There are many in the mountains who behave as if they were in the town, and they are wasting their time. It is better to have many people around you and to live the solitary life in your will, than to be alone and always longing to be with a crowd.'

Abba Isidore said, 'If you fast regularly, do not be inflated with pride; if you think highly of yourself because of it, then you had better eat meat. It is better for a man to eat meat than to be inflated with pride and glorify himself.'

STORY

When blessed Antony was praying in his cell, a voice spoke to him, saying, 'Antony, you have not yet come to the measure of the tanner who is in Alexandria.' When he heard this, the old man arose and took his stick and hurried into the city. When he had found the tanner, he said to him, 'Tell me about your work, for today I have left the desert and come here to see you.'

He replied, 'I am not aware that I have done anything good. When I get up in the morning, before I sit down to work, I say that the whole of this city, small and great, will go into the Kingdom of God because of their good deeds, while I alone will go into eternal punishment because of my evil deeds. Every evening I repeat the same words and believe them in my heart.'

When blessed Antony heard this he said, 'My son, you sit in your own house and work well, and you have the peace of the Kingdom of God; but I spend all my time in solitude with no distractions, and I have not come near the measure of such words.'

Hospitality

SAYINGS

Once three brothers came to visit an old man in Scetis and one of them said to him, 'Abba, I have committed to memory the Old and New Testaments.' And the old man answered, 'You have filled the air with words.' The second one said to him, 'I have written out the Old and New Testaments with my own hand.' He said, 'And you have filled the window-ledge with manuscripts.' Then the third said, 'The grass is growing up my chimney.' And the old man replied, 'You have driven away hospitality.'

Once two brothers came to a certain old man. It was his custom not to eat every day but when he saw them he received them joyfully and said, 'A fast has its own reward, but he who eats for the sake of love fulfils two commandments: he leaves his own will and he refreshes his brothers.'

Abba James said, 'It is better to receive hospitality than to give it.'

STORIES

A brother came to see a certain hermit and, as he was leaving, he said, 'Forgive me, abba, for preventing you from keeping your rule.' The hermit replied, 'My rule is to welcome you with hospitality and to send you away in peace.'

It was said of an old man that he dwelt in Syria on the way to the desert. This was his work: whenever a monk came from the desert, he gave him refreshment with all his heart. Now one day a hermit came and he offered him refreshment. The other did not want to accept it, saying he was fasting. Filled with sorrow, the old man said to him, 'Do not despise your servant, I beg you, do not despise me, but let us pray together. Look at the tree which is here; we will follow the way of whichever of us causes it to bend when he kneels on the ground and prays.' So the hermit knelt down to pray and nothing happened. Then the hospitable one knelt down and at once the tree bent towards him. Taught by this, they gave thanks to God.

Gentleness

SAYINGS

Abba Nilus said, 'Prayer is the seed of gentleness and the absence of anger.'

We came from Palestine to Egypt and went to see one of the fathers. He offered us hospitality and we said, 'Why do you not keep the fast when visitors come to see you? In Palestine they keep it.' He replied, 'Fasting is always with me but I cannot always have you here. It is useful and necessary to fast but we choose whether we will fast or not. What God commands is perfect love. I receive Christ in you and so I must do everything possible to serve you with love. When I have sent you on your way, then I can continue my rule of fasting. The friends of the Bridegroom cannot fast while the Bridegroom is with them; when he is taken away from them, then they will fast.'

STORIES

A hunter in the desert saw abba Antony enjoying himself with the brothers, and he was shocked. Wanting to show him that it was necessary sometimes to meet the needs of the brothers, the old man said to him, 'Put an arrow in your bow and shoot it.' So he did. And the old man said, 'Shoot another,' and he did so. Then the old man said, 'Shoot yet again,' and the hunter replied, 'If I bend my bow so much, I will break it.' Then the old man said to him, 'It is the same with the work of God. If we stretch the brothers beyond measure, they will soon break. Sometimes it is necessary to come down to meet their needs.'

Some monks came to see abba Poemen and said to him, 'When we see brothers dozing during the services in church, should we rouse them so that they can be watchful?' He said to them, 'For my part, when I see a brother dozing, I put his head on my knees and let him rest.'

Beasts and Saints

SAYINGS

Abba Antony said, 'Obedience with abstinence gives men control over wild beasts.'

Abba Theon ate vegetables, but only those that did not need to be cooked. They say that he used to go out of his cell at night and stay in the company of the wild animals, giving them drink from the water he had. Certainly one could see the tracks of antelopes and wild asses and gazelles and other animals near his hermitage. These creatures always gave him pleasure.

Once when a hippopotamus was ravaging the neighbouring countryside the fathers called on abba Bes to help them. He stood at the place and waited and when he saw the beast, which was of enormous size, he commanded it not to ravage the countryside any more, saying, 'In the name of Jesus Christ, I order you not to ravage this countryside anymore.' The hippopotamus vanished completely from that district as if driven away by an angel.

Abba Xanthios said, 'A dog is better than I am, for he has love and he does not judge.'

STORIES

We came near to a tree, led by our kindly host, and there we stumbled upon a lion. At the sight of him my guide and I quaked, but the saintly old man went unfalteringly on and we followed, timorously enough. The wild beast—you would say it was at the command of God—modestly withdrew a little way and sat down, while the old man plucked the fruit from the lower branches. He held out his hand, full of dates; and up the creature ran and took them as frankly as any tame animal about the house; and when it had finished eating, it went away. We stood watching and trembling; reflecting, as well we might, what valour of faith was in him and what poverty of spirit in us.

While abba Macarius was praying in his cave in the desert, a hyena suddenly appeared and began to lick his feet, and taking him gently by the hem of his tunic, she drew him towards her own cave. He followed her, saying, 'I wonder what this animal wants me to do?' When she had led him to her cave, she went in and brought out her cubs which had been born blind. He prayed over them and returned them to the hyena with their sight healed. She in turn, by way of thank-offering, brought the man the huge skin of a ram and laid it at his feet. He smiled at her as if at a kind and sensitive person and taking the skin spread it under him.

Joy

SAYINGS

Amma Syncletica said, 'In the beginning there are a great many battles and a good deal of suffering for those who are advancing towards God and, afterwards, ineffable joy. It is like those who wish to light a fire. At first they are choked with smoke and cry, until they obtain what they seek. As it is said, "Our God is a consuming fire" (Heb. 12: 24); so we also must kindle the divine fire in ourselves through tears and hard work.'

Abba Hyperichius said, 'Praise God continually with spiritual hymns and always remain in meditation and in this way you will be able to bear the burden of the temptations that come upon you. A traveller who is carrying a heavy load pauses from time to time and draws in deep breaths; it makes the journey easier and the burden lighter.'

Abba Elias said, 'If the spirit does not sing with the body, labour is in vain. Whoever loves tribulation will obtain joy and peace later on.'

STORY

When abba Apollo heard the sound of singing from the monks who welcomed us, he greeted us according to the custom which all monks follow. He first lay prostrate on the ground, then got up and kissed us and having brought us in he prayed for us; then, after washing our feet with his own hands, he invited us to partake of some refreshment.

One could see his monks were filled with joy and a bodily contentment such as one cannot see on earth. For nobody among them was gloomy or downcast.

If anyone did appear a little downcast, abba Apollo at once asked him the reason and told each one what was in the secret recesses of his heart. He used to say, 'Those who are going to inherit the Kingdom of Heaven must not be despondent about their salvation.

We who have been considered worthy of so great a hope, how shall we not rejoice without ceasing, since the Apostle urges us always, "Pray without ceasing; in everything give thanks"'

Love

SAYINGS

Abba Poemen said, 'There is no greater love than that a man lays down his life for his neighbour. When you hear someone complaining and you struggle with yourself and do not answer him back with complaints; when you are hurt and bear it patiently, not looking for revenge; then you are laying down your life for your neighbour.'

One of the beloved of Christ who had the gift of mercy used to say, 'The one who is filled with mercy ought to offer it in the same manner in which he has received it, for such is the mercy of God.'

Abba Antony said, 'I no longer fear God, I love him; for love casts out fear.'

STORIES

Abba Agathon said, 'If I could meet a leper, give him my body and take his, I should be very happy.' That is perfect charity. It was also said of him that when he came into the town one day to sell his goods, he met a sick traveller lying in the public place with no one to care for him. The old man rented a room and lived with him there, working with his hands to pay the rent and spending the rest of the money on the sick man's needs. He stayed there four months until the sick man was well again. Then he went back to his cell in peace.

A soldier asked abba Mios if God accepted repentance. After the old man had taught him many things, he said, 'Tell me, my dear, if your cloak is torn, do you throw it away?' He replied, 'No, I mend it and use it again.' The old man said to him, 'If you are so careful about your cloak, will not God be equally careful about his creature?'

God is for All

SAYINGS

God is the life of all free beings. He is the salvation of all, of believers or unbelievers, of the just or the unjust, of the pious or the impious, of those freed from passions or those caught up in them, of monks or those living in the world, of the educated or the illiterate, of the healthy or the sick, of the young or the very old. He is like the outpouring of light, the glimpse of the sun, or the changes of the weather which are the same for everyone without exception.

Abba Pambo said, 'If you have a heart, you can be saved.'

STORY

There was an old man living in the desert who served God for many years and he said, 'Lord, let me know if I have pleased you.' He saw an angel who said to him, 'You have not yet become like the gardener in such and such a place.' The old man marvelled and said, 'I will go off to the city to see both him and what it is that he does that surpasses all my work and toil of all these years.'

So he went to the city and asked the gardener about his way of life. ... When they were getting ready to eat in the evening, the old man heard people in the streets singing songs, for the cell of the gardener was in a public place. Therefore the old man said to him, 'Brother, wanting as you do to live according to God, how do you remain in this place and not be troubled when you hear them singing these songs?'

The man said, 'I tell you, abba, I have never been troubled or scandalized.' When he heard this the old man said, 'What, then, do you think in your heart when you hear these things?' And he replied, 'That they are all going into the Kingdom.' When he heard this, the old man marvelled and said, 'This is the practice which surpasses my labour of all these years.'

Love of God

Prayer

SAYINGS

They asked abba Macarius, 'How should we pray?' And the old man replied, 'There is no need to speak much in prayer; often stretch out your hands and say, "Lord, as you will and as you know, have mercy on me." But if there is war in your soul, add, "Help me!" and because he knows what we need, he shows mercy on us.'

Abba Lot went to see abba Joseph and he said to him, 'Abba, as far as I can, I say my little office, I fast a little, I pray and meditate, I live in peace and as far as I can I purify my thoughts. What else can I do?' Then the old man stood up and stretched his hands towards heaven; his fingers became like ten lamps of fire and he said to him, 'If you will, you can become all flame.'

Abba Paul said, 'Keep close to Jesus.'

STORY

Some monks came to see abba Lucius and they said to him, 'We do not work with our hands; we obey Paul's command and pray without ceasing.' The old man said, 'Do you not eat or sleep?' They said, 'Yes, we do.' He said, 'Who prays for you while you are asleep? … Excuse me, brothers, but you do not practise what you claim. I will show you how I pray without ceasing, though I work with my hands.'

'With God's help, I collect a few palm-leaves and sit down and weave them, saying, "Have mercy upon me, O God, after thy great goodness; according to the multitude of thy mercies do away with mine offences."' He said to them, 'Is this prayer or not?' They said, 'Yes, it is.'

And he continued, 'When I have worked and prayed in my heart all day, I make about sixteen pence. Two of these I put outside my door and with the rest I buy food. And he who finds the two coins outside the door prays for me while I eat and sleep. And so by the help of God I pray without ceasing.'

Intercession

SAYINGS

It is clear to all who dwell in Egypt that it is through the monks that the world is kept in being and that through them also human life is preserved and honoured by God. … There is no town or village in Egypt that is not surrounded by hermitages as if by walls, and all the people depend on the prayers of the monks as if on God himself.

Palladius said, 'One day when I was suffering from boredom I went to abba Macarius and said, "What shall I do? My thoughts afflict me, saying, you are not making any progress, go away from here."' He said to me, 'Tell them, for Christ's sake I am guarding the walls.'

STORY

Abba Macarius said, 'Walking one day in the desert, I found the skull of a dead man lying on the ground. As I was moving it with my stick, the skull spoke to me. I said to it, "Who are you?" The skull replied, "I was the high priest of the idols and of the pagans who dwelt in this place; but you are Macarius, the Spirit-bearer. Whenever you take pity on those who are in torment and pray for them they feel a little respite."'

The old man said to him, 'What is this alleviation, and what is this torment?' He said to him, 'As far as the sky is removed from the earth, so great is the fire beneath us. We are standing in the midst of the fire from the feet up to the head. It is not possible to see anyone face to face, but the face of one is fixed to the back of another. Yet when you pray for us, each of us can see the other's face a little; such is our respite.'

The Cell

SAYINGS

The monk's cell is like the furnace of Babylon where the three children found the Son of God, and it is like the pillar of cloud where God spoke with Moses.

A certain brother came to abba Moses in Scetis, seeking a word from him, and the old man said to him, 'Go and sit in your cell and your cell will teach you everything.'

Abba Antony said, 'Just as fish die if they stay out of water, so monks who tarry outside their cells or in the company of worldly men move away from their desire for solitude. Fish can only live in the sea, and so we must hurry back to our cells in case by staying outside we forget to care for what is inside.'

STORIES

Amma Theodora said, 'There was a monk who, because of the great number of his temptations, said, "I will go away from here." As he was putting on his sandals, he saw another man who was also putting on his sandals and this man said to him, "Is it on account of me that you are going away? Because I will go before you, wherever you are going."'

An old man came to the cell of abba John and he found him asleep, with an angel standing by him, fanning him.

Constant Prayer

SAYINGS

A brother said to a father, 'If I accidentally oversleep and am late beginning my prayers, I am ashamed and in case the others hear me beginning to pray late, I become very reluctant to begin to pray at all.' The old man said to him, 'If ever you oversleep in the early morning, get up the moment you wake, shut the door and the windows and begin the prayers as usual. For it is written, "The day is thine and the night is thine." God is glorified whatever time it is.'

Abba Agathon said, 'There is no labour greater than prayer to God. For every time someone wants to pray, his enemies the demons want to prevent him, for they know that it is only by turning him from prayer that they can hinder his journey. Whatever good work a man undertakes, if he perseveres in it he will attain rest. But prayer is warfare to the last breath.'

When a monk stands in prayer, if he prays alone, he does not pray at all.

STORIES

Amma Theodora said, 'It is good to live in peace for so the wise man can practise perpetual prayer. But as soon as your intention is to live in peace, at once the evil one comes and weighs down your soul. But this is how to meet him: there was a monk who was seized by cold and fever every time he began to pray and he also suffered from headaches. In this condition he said to himself, "I am ill and near to death; so now is the time to get up and pray before I die." When he had done this, the fever vanished. So by reasoning in this way the brother resisted and prayed and was able to control his thoughts.'

It was said of abba Arsenius that on Saturday evenings, preparing for the glory of Sunday, he would turn his back on the sun and stretch out his hands in prayer towards the heavens, till once again the sun shone on his face; then he would sit down.

Many Mansions

A brother asked an old man, 'What thing is there so good that I may do it and live?' And the old man said, 'God alone knows what is good. … the Scriptures say that Abraham was hospitable and God was with him; and David was humble and God was with him. Therefore, what you find your soul desires in following God, do it and keep your heart set on him.'

Abba Poemen related that abba John said that the saints are like a group of trees, each bearing different fruit, but watered from the same source. The practices of one saint differ from those of another, but it is the same Spirit that works in all of them.

STORY

A brother came to Scetis to see abba Arsenius. Having knocked on the door, the visitor and the monk who was with him entered; the old man greeted them and they sat down without saying anything.

The brother from the church said, 'I will leave you; pray for me.' But the visiting brother did not feel at ease with the old man and said, 'I will come with you,' so they left together.

Then the visitor said, 'Take me to abba Moses who used to be a robber.' When they arrived, the father welcomed them joyfully and then took leave of them with delight. …

That night the father prayed to God, saying, 'Lord, explain this matter to me; for thy name's sake one flees from men, and the other for thy name's sake receives them with open arms.' Then two large boats were shown him on the river, and he saw abba Arsenius and the Spirit of God sailing in one in perfect peace; and in the other was abba Moses with the angels of God, and they were all eating honey cakes.'

Stability

SAYINGS

A brother asked an old man, 'What shall I do, father, for I am not acting like a monk at all, but I eat, drink and sleep, carelessly, and I have evil thoughts and I am in great trouble, passing from one work to another and from that work to the next.' The old man said, 'Sit in your cell and do the little you can, untroubled. For I think the little you can do now is of equal value to the great deeds which abba Antony accomplished on the mountain and I believe that by remaining in your cell for the name of God and guarding your conscience, you also will find the place where abba Antony is.'

Sarapion the Sindonite travelled once on a pilgrimage to Rome. Here he was told of a celebrated recluse, a woman who lived always in one small room, never going out. Sceptical about her way of life—for he was himself a great wanderer—Sarapion called on her and asked, 'Why are you sitting here?' To which she replied, 'I am not sitting; I am on a journey.'

STORY

There were three friends … and the first chose to reconcile those who were fighting against each other, as it is said, 'Blessed are the peacemakers.' The second chose to visit the sick. The third went to live in prayer and stillness in the desert.

Now in spite of all his labours, the first could not make peace in all men's quarrels, and in his sorrow he went to the one who was serving the sick and found him also disheartened.

So they went to see the one who was living in stillness and prayer and told him their difficulties. After a short silence he poured water into a bowl and said to them, 'Look at the water', and it was disturbed. After a while he said 'Look again', and they could see their faces reflected in the still water.

Then he said, 'It is the same for those who live among men; disturbance prevents them from seeing their faults; but when a man is still, then he sees his failings.'

Temptation

SAYINGS

It is related of amma Sarah that for thirteen years she waged warfare against the demon of fornication. She never prayed that the warfare should cease but she said, 'O God, give me strength.'

Just as no one can cause harm to someone who is close to a king, no more can Satan do anything to us if our souls are close to God, for he said truly, 'Draw near to me and I will be near to you.' But since we often exalt ourselves, the enemy has no difficulty in drawing our souls towards shameful passions.

The greatest thing a man can do is to throw his faults before the Lord and expect temptation to his last breath.

STORY

It happened that abba Moses was struggling with the temptation of fornication. Unable to stay any longer in the cell, he went and told abba Isidore. The old man exhorted him to return to his cell but he refused, saying, 'Abba, I cannot.'

Then abba Isidore took abba Moses out onto the terrace and said to him, 'Look towards the West.' He looked and saw hordes of demons flying about and making a noise before launching an attack.

Then abba Isidore said to him, 'Look towards the East.' He turned and saw an innumerable multitude of holy angels shining with glory.

Abba Isidore said, 'See, these are sent by the Lord to the saints to bring them help, while those in the West fight against them. Those that are with us are more in number than they are.'

Then abba Moses gave thanks to God, plucked up courage and returned to his cell.

The Single Eye

SAYINGS

On a journey a monk met some nuns, and when he saw them he turned aside from the road. The abbess said to him, 'If you had been a perfect monk, you would not have looked at us and you would not have known that we were women.'

When he was dying, abba Bessarion said, 'The monk should be like the cherubim and seraphim: all eye.'

Someone asked abba Antony, 'What must one do in order to please God?' The old man replied, 'Pay attention to what I tell you: whoever you may be, always have God before your eyes; whatever you do, do it according to the testimony of the holy Scriptures; in whatever place you live, do not readily leave it. Keep these three precepts and you will be saved.'

STORIES

Once a priest from Scetis went to see the bishop of Alexandria. When he came back to Scetis, the brothers asked him, 'How are things in the city?' He said to them, 'Believe me, brethren, I did not see anyone there except the bishop.' When they heard this, they wondered and said, 'What do you think has happened to all the people?' for they hesitated to believe him. But the priest reassured them, saying, 'I had wrestled with my soul so as not to look on the face of man.' So the brothers were edified and controlled themselves about raising their eyes.

A brother came to the cell of abba Arsenius. Waiting outside the door, he saw that the old man had become entirely like a flame. When he knocked, the old man came out and saw the brother marvelling. He said to him, 'Have you been knocking long? Did you see anything here?' The brother answered, 'No.' So he talked with him and sent him away.

True Learning

SAYINGS

Epiphanius the bishop said, 'The acquisition of Christian books is necessary for those who can use them; for the very sight of them renders us less inclined to sin and incites us to believe more firmly in righteousness.'

Abba Antony said, 'Fear not this goodness as a thing impossible, nor the pursuit of it as something alien, set a great way off; it hangs on our own choice. For the sake of Greek learning, men go overseas. ... But the City of God has its foundations in every seat of human habitation. ... The Kingdom of God is within. The goodness that is in us asks only the human mind.'

STORIES

One day, abba Arsenius consulted an old Egyptian monk about his thoughts. Someone noticed this and said to him, 'Abba Arsenius, how is it that you, with such a good Latin and Greek education, ask this peasant about your thoughts?' He replied, 'I have indeed been taught Latin and Greek, but I do not even know the alphabet of this peasant.'

A certain philosopher questioned the holy Antony, 'How can you be content, father, without the comfort of books?' He replied, 'My book, O philosopher, is the nature of created things, and whenever I wish to read the words of God, it is in my hand.'

Scripture

SAYINGS

Abba Amoun (of the place called Raythu) came to abba Sisois with this question: 'When I read Scripture, I long to prepare elaborate comments, so that I will be ready to answer questions about it if I am asked.' The old man said, 'There is no need. It is better to speak the word simply, with a good conscience and a pure mind.'

Abba Amoun asked abba Antony, 'When I talk to my neighbour, should we speak about the Scriptures or the sayings of the Fathers?' The old man answered him, 'If you cannot be silent, you had better talk about the sayings of the Fathers than about the Scriptures; it is not so dangerous.'

Bishop Epiphanius said, 'Ignorance of the Scriptures is a precipice and a deep abyss.'

STORIES

Once some of the old men came to abba Antony and abba Joseph was among them. Abba Antony wanted to test them, and so he began to talk about the Holy Scriptures. He began asking the younger monks the meaning of one text after another and each replied as best he could. But he said to each of them, 'You have not found the meaning of it yet.' Then he said to abba Joseph, 'What do you say this text means?' and he answered, 'I do not know.' Abba Antony said, 'Indeed, only abba Joseph has found the true way, when he said he did not know.'

Abba Antony said, 'Wherever you may be, have God always before your eyes; whatever you do, do it according to the testimony of Holy Scripture; in whatever place you live, do not readily leave it.'

The Cross

SAYINGS

I was sitting one day with abba Poemen and I saw him in an ecstasy and, as I was on terms of great freedom with him, I begged him saying, 'Tell me where you were.' He was forced to answer and he said, 'My thoughts were with St Mary, the Mother of God, as she wept by the cross of the Saviour; I would that I would always weep like that.'

Abba Hyperichius said, 'The true service of a monk is obedience and if he has this, whatever he asks will be given him and he will stand with confidence before the Crucified. For that was how the Lord went to his cross, being made obedient even unto death.'

An old man said, 'Joseph of Arimathea took the body of Jesus and placed it in a clean garment within a new tomb, which signifies a new humanity. Therefore let each one strive attentively not to sin so that he does not mistreat the God who dwells within him and drive him away from his soul.'

STORIES

A brother asked an old man, 'How can I be saved?' The latter took off his habit, girded his loins and raised his hands towards heaven, saying, 'So should a monk be, denuded of all things of this world, and crucified. In the contest the athlete fights with his fists; in his thoughts the monk stands, his arms stretched out in the form of a cross to heaven, calling on God. The athlete stands naked when fighting in a contest; the monk stands naked and stripped of all things, anointed with oil and taught by his Master how to fight. So God leads us to the victory.'

A monk and a nun made it their custom to visit a hermit at the same time. Seeing what was happening, when they came in, the old man lay down and went to sleep. They were attacked by lust and they sinned. … As they were going away they wondered if the old man knew or not. So they went back to the old man and repented and asked him, 'Father, did you not know how Satan mocked us?' He said to them, 'Yes, indeed.' They replied, 'Where were your thoughts at the time?' He said to them, 'At the time, my mind was where Christ was crucified, and I was standing there weeping.'

Tears

SAYINGS

A brother asked abba Poemen, 'What can I do about my sins?' And the old man answered him, 'Weep interiorly, for both deliverance from faults and the acquisition of virtues are gained through compunction. Weeping is the way the Scriptures and the Fathers have handed on to us.'

A brother said to an old man, 'I hear the old men weeping and my soul longs for tears, but they do not come and my soul is troubled.' And the elder said, 'The children of Israel entered the promised land. If you have reached them, you will no longer be afraid of the conflict. For God wills that the soul be afflicted thus, that it may always be longing to enter that country.'

STORIES

Athanasius of holy memory asked abba Pambo to come down to Alexandria from the desert. When he arrived he saw there a woman who was an actress, and he wept. When he was asked by those standing by why he was weeping, he said, 'Two things move me: one is her condemnation, the other is that I do not take as much trouble to please God as she does to please the worst of mankind.'

It was said of abba Arsenius that he had a hollow in his chest channelled out by the tears which fell from his eyes all his life while he sat at his manual work. When abba Poemen learned that he was dead, he said, weeping, 'Truly you are blessed, abba Arsenius, for you wept for yourself in this world! He who does not weep for himself here below will weep eternally hereafter; so it is impossible not to weep, either voluntarily or when compelled through suffering.'

Death

SAYINGS

It was said of abba Sisoes that when he was at the point of death, while the Fathers were sitting around him, his face shone like the sun. He said to them, 'Look, abba Antony is coming.' A little later on he said, 'Look, the choir of prophets is coming.' Again his countenance shone with brightness and he said, 'Look, the choir of apostles is coming.'

His countenance increased in brightness and he spoke with someone. The old men asked him, 'With whom are you speaking, father?' He said, 'The angels have come to fetch me and I am begging them to let me stay and do a little penance.' The old men said to him, 'You have no need to do penance, father.' But the old man said to them, 'Truly, I do not think I have even made a beginning yet.'

Once more his countenance suddenly became like the sun and they were all filled with fear. He said to them, 'Look, the Lord is coming and he is saying, "Bring me the vessel from the desert."' Then there came a flash of lightning and all the house was filled with a sweet odour.

STORIES

When abba Agathon was at the point of death … the brothers wanted to ask him many questions but he said to them, 'If you love me, do not talk to me any more for I do not have any more time.' So he died with joy and they saw him departing like one greeting his dearest friends.

They used to say about abba Pambo that when he left this life he said to the old men standing around him, 'From the time I came into this solitude and built myself a cell and lived in it, I do not remember having eaten anything that my hand had not worked for nor have I regretted a word spoken until now. And so I go to the Lord as one who has not yet made a beginning of serving him.'

Repentance

SAYINGS

It was said of a brother that his thoughts suggested to him, 'Relax today and tomorrow repent.' But he retorted, 'No, I am going to repent today and may the will of God be done tomorrow.'

Some brothers said, 'When we listened to the words of our father, Pachomius, we were greatly helped and spurred on with zeal for good works; we saw how, even when he kept silence, he taught by his actions. We were amazed by him and we used to say to each other, "We thought that all the saints were created as saints by God … and we thought that sinners could not live devoutly because they had not been created good. But we see the goodness of God manifested in our father, for he is of pagan origin and he has become devout; he has put on all the commandments of God. Thus even we also can follow him and become equal to the saints whom he himself has followed, as it is written, Come unto me, all ye that labour and are heavy laden and I will give you rest (Matt. 11: 28)."'

STORIES

Two brothers went to market to sell the things they had made. The first fell into the sin of fornication as soon as he separated from his companion. He met his brother, who said to him, 'My brother, let us return to our cell.' But he said, 'I am not going.' The other persisted, saying, 'My brother, why not?' He said, 'Because when you had left me, I sinned by fornication.' His brother, wanting to help him, said, 'The same thing happened to me, too, when you left me; come, and let us go and do penance and God will forgive us.' They went and told the old men what had happened to them and they were given a penance; so one of the brothers did the same penance, as though he himself had also sinned, and God, seeing the affliction he had undertaken for love's sake, forgave his brother. This is what it means to give one's life for one's brother.

Abba Apollo had sinned very gravely but his heart was filled with compunction … and he passed all his time in prayer, saying, 'I, as man, have sinned; do thou, as God, forgive.'

True Miracles

SAYINGS

Abba Pachomius said, 'A sinner like me does not ask God that he may see visions, for that is against his will, and wrong. Hear all the same about a great miracle: if you see a man pure and humble, that is a great vision; for what is greater than such a vision, to see the invisible God in his temple, a visible man?'

Abba Euprepios said, 'Knowing that God is faithful and mighty, have faith in him and you will share what is his. If you are depressed, you do not believe. We all believe that he is mighty and believe that everything is possible to him. As for your own affairs, believe with faith in him about them, too, for he is able to work miracles in you also.'

STORIES

The devil appeared to a monk, disguised as an angel of light, and said to him, 'I am the angel Gabriel and I have been sent to you.' But the monk said, 'See if you have not been sent to someone else; I am not worthy to have an angel sent to me.' And at once the devil vanished.

It was said of an old man that while he was sitting in his cell and striving he saw the demons visibly and he scorned them. The devil, seeing himself overcome, came and showed himself to him saying, 'In fact, I am Christ.' When he saw him, the old man closed his eyes and the devil said to him, 'Why are you closing your eyes? I am Christ.' And the old man answered him, 'I do not want to see Christ here below.' And the devil vanished.

Three monks met unexpectedly at the river bank and one of them said, 'I ask as a gift from God that we should arrive at our destination without fatigue in the power of the Spirit.' Scarcely had he prayed when a boat was found ready to sail together with a favourable wind, and in the twinkling of an eye they found themselves at their destination, although they were travelling upstream.

Sources

Lives: *Lives of the Desert Fathers,* trans. Norman Russell, Cistercian Publications 1980/88.

PL: *Patrologia Latina* LXXIII, Verba Seniorum cols. 855-1022 (Benedicta Ward's translation).

Sayings: *Sayings of the Desert Fathers; the Alphabetic Collection,* trans. Benedicta Ward, Cistercian Publications 1975/83.

Wisdom: *Wisdom of the Desert Fathers,* trans. Benedicta Ward, SLG Press 1986.

World: *World of the Desert Fathers,* trans. Columba Stewart OSB, SLG Press 1986.

Thanks are due to Cistercian Publications for kind permission to use extracts from the publications listed above, New Directions **10(d)**, Paulist Press **20(a)**, **25(b)**, **30(b)**.

The figures in bold type refer to the pages of readings in this book. They are followed by the Sources.

'Prayer from the Desert' is taken from *Western Asceticism* by Owen Chadwick (London, SCM Press 1958), pp. 188-9.

1   (a) *World* XXVI (92), p. 36.

    (b) *Sayings* Macarius 32, p. 134.

    (c) *PL* IX, 10: col. 911.

    (d) *PL* IX, 6: col. 910.

    (e) *Sayings* Moses 2, p. 117.

    (f) *Sayings* Bessarion 7, p. 35.

2   (a) *Sayings* Isidore the Priest 2, p. 2.

    (b) *Sayings* Nisteros 3, p. 130.

    (c) *Wisdom* 221, p. 60.

    (d) *Sayings* Poemen 191, p. 163.

3   (a) *PL* XIV, 9: cols. 949-50.

    (b) *Wisdom* 15, p. 45.

    (c) *Sayings* Mios 1, p. 127.

    (d) *Sayings* Mark 1, p. 123.

5   (a) *PL* X, 111: col. 932.

    (b) *Sayings* Ammoe 2, p. 26.

    (c) *Sayings* Sylvanus 11, p. 188.

    (d) *Sayings* John the Dwarf 2, p. 73.

    (e) *Sayings* John the Dwarf 37, p. 79.

6   (a) *PL* XV, 82: col. 1967.

(b) *Wisdom* 166, p. 47.

(c) *Sayings* Macarius the Great 11, pp. 109–10.

(d) *Wisdom* 117, p. 49.

7　(a) *PL* VI, 6: col. 889.

(b) *Sayings* Syncletica 5, p. 194.

(c) *PL* XVI, 6: col. 970.

(d) *PL* V, 20: col. 892.

(e) *PL* V, 3: col. 888.

9　(a) *PL* XIV, 10: col. 950.

(b) *Sayings* Antony 9, p. 2.

(c) *Sayings* Poemen 159, p. 159.

(d) *World* 5, VIII (62), p.20.

(e) *Sayings* Isaiah 3, p. 59.

10　(a) *Sayings* Arsenius 1 and 2, p. 8.

(b) *PL* II, 9: col. 859.

(c) *PL* II, 11: col. 859.

(d) *Wisdom of the Desert,* trans. Thomas Merton (New York, New
Directions, 1970), paperback edn, p. 73, no. cxxx.

(e) *Lives* XX, 8, Nitria, pp. 148–9.

11　(a) *Sayings* Antony 24, p. 5.

(b) *PL* II, 14: col. 860.

(c) *Sayings* Isidore the Priest 4, p. 91.

(d) *PL* XV, 2: col. 1038.

12　(a) *Wisdom* 153, p. 43.

(b) *PL* XIII, 7: col. 945.

(c) *Sayings* James 1, p. 89.

(d) *PL* XII, 7: col. 943.

(e) *Wisdom* 153, p. 43.

14　(a) *Sayings* Nilus 2, p. 129.

(b) *PL* XIII, 2: cols. 943–4.

(c) *Sayings* Antony 13, p. 3.

(d) *Sayings* Poemen 92, p. 151.

15　(a) *Sayings* Antony 36, p. 7.

(b) *Lives* VI, Theon 4, p. 68.

(c) *Lives* IV, Bes 2, p. 66.

(d) *Sayings* Xanthios 3, p. 134.

(e) Helen Waddell, *Beasts and Saints* (London, Constable 1934), pp. 4–5.

(f) *Lives* XXI, Macarius 15, p. 110.

17　(a) *Sayings* Syncletica 1, p. 193.

(b) *PL* VII, 20: col. 897.

(c) *Sayings* Elias 6, p. 61.

(d) *Lives* VIII, Apollo 48, pp. 77–8.

19 (a) *PL* XVII, 10: cols. 971–2.

(b) *World* 2, III (40), p. 33.

(c) *Sayings* Antony 32, p. 6.

(d) *Sayings* Agathon 26 and 27, p. 20.

(e) *Sayings* Mios 3, p. 127.

20 (a) John Climacus, *The Ladder of Divine Ascent*, trans. C. Luibheid and N. Russell (London, SPCK 1982), p. 74.

(b) *Sayings* Pambo 10, p. 66.

(c) *World* 2, XI (67), pp. 12–13.

23 (a) *PL* XII, 10: col. 942.

(b) *Sayings* Joseph of Panephysis 7, p. 88.

(c) *Sayings* Paul the Great 4, p. 172

(d) *PL* XII, 9: col. 942.

25 (a) *Lives* Prologue 9 and 10, p. 50.

(b) Palladius, *The Lausiac History*, trans. R. T. Meyer (New York, Paulist Press, 1965), p. 67.

(c) *Sayings* Macarius the Great 38, pp. 115–16.

26 (a) *Wisdom* 74, p. 24.

(b) *PL* II, 9: col. 859.

(c) *Sayings* Antony 10, p. 2.

(d) *Sayings* Theodora 7, p. 71.

(e) *Sayings* John the Dwarf 33, p. 78.

27 (a) *PL* X, 98: col. 893.

(b) *Sayings* Agathon 9, p. 18.

(c) *World* 11, XXXIII (104), p. 37.

(d) *Sayings* Theodora 3, p. 71.

(e) *Sayings* Arsenius 30, p. 12.

29 (a) *PL* I, 2: col. 956.

(b) *Sayings* John the Dwarf 34, p. 95.

(c) *Sayings* Arsenius 38, p. 15.

30 (a) *PL* VII, 34: col. 901.

(b) Palladius, *The Lausiac History*, trans. R. T. Meyer (New York, Paulist Press, 1965), pp. 108–9.

(c) *Wisdom* 2, p. 1.

32 (a) *Sayings* Sarah 1, p. 192.

(b) *Wisdom* 136, p. 39.

(c) *Sayings* Antony 4, p. 2.

(d) *Sayings* Moses 1, p. 138.

33 (a) *Sayings* Antony 3, p. 2.

(b) *PL* IV, 62: col. 872.

(c) *PL* XI, 7: col. 934.

(d) *PL* IV, 55: col. 871.

(e) *Sayings* Arsenius 27, p. 11.

34 (a) *Sayings* Epiphanius 8, p. 49.

(b) Helen Waddell, *The Desert Fathers* (London, Constable, 1936/72) p. 7.

(c) *Sayings* Arsenius 6, p. 18.

(d) *PL* XXI, 16: col. 1018.

35 (a) *PL* VIII, 16: col. 908.

(b) *Sayings* Amoun of Nitria 2, p. 27.

(c) *Sayings* Epiphanius 11, p. 49.

(d) *Sayings* Antony 17, pp. 3–4.

(e) *Sayings* Antony 3, p. 2.

36 (a) *Sayings* Poemen 144, p. 157.

(b) *Sayings* Hyperichius 8, p. 200.

(c) *World* 2, I (24), p. 33.

(d) *Wisdom* 11, p. 3.

(e) *World* 6, III (13) p. 22.

38 (a) *Sayings* Poemen 208 and 209, p. 164.

(b) *PL* III, 27: col. 864.

(c) *PL* III, 14: col. 862.

(d) *Sayings* Arsenius 41, p. 16.

39 (a) *Sayings* Sisoes 14, p. 21.

(b) *Sayings* Agathon 29, p. 214–15.

(c) *PL* I, 16: col. 857.

40 (a) *Sayings* Psenthaisios 1, p. 205.

(b) *Wisdom* 139, p. 40.

(c) *Wisdom* 47, p. 15.

(d) *Sayings* Apollo 2, p. 31.

42 (a) *Pachomian Koinonia,* trans. Armand Veilleux (Kalamazoo, Cistercian Publications, 1980), vol. 1, 'The Greek Life of Pachomius' 48, p. 330.

(b) *Sayings* Euprepios 1, p. 52.

(c) *Wisdom* 178, p. 50.

(d) *Wisdom* 180, p. 50.

(e) *Lives* XI, Sourous, p. 88.